Listen, Love...!

31 Days and a Wake-up

My Journey Back to Freedom

April Nachelle Barksdale

DEDICATION

This book is dedicated first and foremost to my amazing husband **Bernard** and my children **Jalen, Jasmine, and Jayla**. Your support, dedication, and belief in me and my dreams have helped me regain all that prison attempted to strip away. All that I am and all that I become is because of your unconditional love.

To **South Carolina Kairos Prison Ministry Volunteers**: I am sorry that I can't acknowledge you all by name. Mere words will never be enough to express my gratitude for what you gave to me. Your willingness to meet those who many consider to be 'the incorrigible of society' right where they are and to remind them of the love that God still has for them in spite of it all is incredible. God knew I needed you to make it through and I am forever grateful for your selfless sacrifice. I was granted true freedom before I was ever released from prison **"BECAUSE OF YOU.**

To the women of **Leath Correctional Institution** in Greenwood, SC who remain behind prison walls; who forever changed who I am. You taught, and are still teaching me how to be strong; how to endure; how to be content in all things; and most of all...how to survive.
Thank you.

To all of my **'Beyond the RazorWire'** family. We made it to the other side and despite the obstacles and challenges we face, we strive to make it together. Thank you for your support and belief in my vision. We are proof that we are not what we have done; but what we have overcome.
We are 'Forever Bonded by the Wire'.

ACKNOWLEDGMENTS

Thank you to Pastor Michael Green for your acceptance, spiritual guidance, friendship and your ability to make me think outside of the box.

Thank you to Charlene Evans a.k.a. Chiccy Baritone for ' Breakfast for Champions'. Your desire to empower women is why this book exists. It was your ministry that challenged me to embrace who I was destined to be and to confidently, boldly, and courageously share my talents and story with the world. I am indebted to you infinitely.

I can't forget to acknowledge a very special group of people; to every person who was used by the enemy in an attempt to stop what God had ordained. The abuse, the heartache, the abandonment, the hurt, the guilt, the betrayals, and the shame that was inflicted by you was for my good....Thanks for making me a fighter

Introduction

You are holding a dream brought to life. This book was written within the confines of prison during one of the hardest, darkest, and most rewarding times of my life. My incarceration can seem contradictory because there was good and bad; highs and lows; happiness and sadness; struggles and triumphs; failures and victories; all of which were necessary for God to complete his work in me.

Throughout this book I express my anger, frustration, and disdain for a system that seems irretrievably broken. In all organizations there is good and evil; and Leath Correctional Institution was no different. My thoughts and words do not represent the institution as a whole.

Correctional officers have difficult jobs; one that is unique in that those they serve are also the ones they have to imprison. Incarceration isn't supposed to be a vacation by any means but, it doesn't have to strip individuals of their dignity in order to be effective.

There were employees of the South Carolina Department of Corrections who through their actions showed that they were only there for a paycheck. There were some who were mean, cruel, and didn't even attempt to treat us (inmates) like we were still humans despite being caged like animals.

Then there were the good ones; those who were firm but fair. They did their jobs by the book, most of the time I didn't understand them at first but I came to respect them because they treated everyone the same and they were consistent.

Then there were those who were genuinely concerned, who didn't break the rules but, they made sure that I knew they cared. They talked to and encouraged me on my difficult days. They listened to my problems and told me that I would make it.

After my release, I had an opportunity to read about 'The Stanford Prison Experiment' and it changed my perspective about the correctional officers who appeared to be the bad apples in the bunch.

To learn more about the 1971 experiment that is still relevant today

Visit http://www.prisonexp.org/

"There is some good in the worst of us and some evil in the best of us. When we discover this, we are less prone to hate our enemies."

-Dr. Martin Luther King, Jr.

CRY FOR FREEDOM

During my darkest nights I find.
Myself calling out for you.
Longing to lie beneath a blanket of stars,
While not confined behind concrete and bars.

I long to see the sunrise, from the other side of these gates.
Oh, how desperately I want to *'escape'*...
But wait, without you, I can't freely use that word;
Without giving an explanation or getting more time, if it was ever heard.

With the promise of you I am stronger.
Capable of seeing, hoping, and dreaming beyond tomorrow.
With you I could express my joy and embrace my deepest sorrows.

Freedom!!!!! Can't you hear me? I've been calling you for five long years.
But, you have eluded me.
And because of your absence I have cried so many tears.

Tears, for the twenty-nine years you were mine.
But, I took you for granted-- time after time.
Tears, because I was stripped of you;
Disenfranchised by the court.
I realized your depth and value in that moment
But, was a day late and a dollar short.

Tears, because, in my dreams, I have you,
And I'm reunited with family and friends...
Only to have you snatched away---as the count bell rings once again.

Freedom!!!!! I promise; when I have you once more;
Everything about you I will adore.
The birds in flight. The moonlit nights.
The mountains in their glorious splendor.
All of your blessings, I will remember.

With you, my days of wearing shackles and chains,
Will have passed me by.
But, until then, I need to know---
Freedom do you hear my cry?

"There is no education like adversity"

-Benjamin Disraeli

July 31st, 2011

Wow! I can't believe that I'm here! When I say "here", I mean, I am finally to the point where I feel comfortable counting the days until I am free once again. Before now, I refused to count days because of the innate fear I had that if I focused too much on my release, the calendar would stop moving. There are people who methodically woke up each day and placed an "x" over the day to signify tem being another step closer to the door but, the only thing I could do was focus on making it through one day at a time. Looking at the whole picture was too much, too heart wrenching, too much to bear, and there were days I wasn't sure I was strong enough to make it through one day...let alone thousands. Even now, my incarceration still seems like a bad dream I will wake up from any minute now.

I actually have butterflies in my stomach tonight because once the people scheduled for release leave in the morning- I'm on deck and the anxiety and anticipation is already building. It's the same feeling I felt on my first day of school; every Christmas Eve (before I found out that Santa didn't really exist); on the night of my 8th grade prom; and the feeling I had just before each of my children were born...all of these emotions rolled into one.

At 3am this morning Alanis Morisette's *"I Will Remember You"*, opened one of the psychological trap doors I created over the years so that I could survive prison without losing my sanity. The trap doors aren't real, they are the places where I have kept my deepest hurts hidden because in prison...crying is a sign of weakness, being emotional is a sign of weakness; it's like dousing yourself with blood and jumping into a shark infested tank and besides, no one really cares in prison anyway.

My grandmother passed away in February 2007. I cried for a short moment in the visitation area where my mom and sister came to break the news but, after that I refused to grieve her death because I didn't think I could handle losing her and deal with all that is associated with surviving from one day to the next when you are behind bars.

Hearing that song opened a floodgate...and I allowed myself to cry. I think I was finally able to let go because in 31 days and a wake-up, I will once again experience freedom beyond the razor wire.

"It is interesting to notice how some minds seem almost to create themselves, springing up under every disadvantage, and working their solitary but irresistible way through a thousand obstacles."

-Washington Irving

31 Days and a Wake-Up   August 1st, 2011

In prison 31 days and a wake-up is our way of saying that we have a month to go and one day (release day) to wake-up here before our ordeal is over. I didn't understand that concept when I first arrived as SC Inmate # 312241-- why couldn't they just say a month? As time progressed, I knew why. Each day you wake up here is another one that belongs to the state and after seeing a number of people reach the gate, only to be turned around before it could be opened to them due to a miscalculation of their time etc. I learned you don't get your heart set on freedom until it is truly yours.

Journaling has been difficult since I have been in prison because I never wanted to remember the trauma that prison inflicted upon my life. I feel like the more memories of this place that I hold onto, the more I become resolved and content with my incarceration. By God's grace, I have discovered peace but, I will never be okay with being here. Some people here act like they are on vacation and I will never understand that. Other inmates have said that I need to relax and stop taking everything so serious but, to me this is serious. Every day that I am away from my children is serious! Every day that I cannot make the smallest decisions concerning myself is serious. Every day that I am without my freedom is serious.

So, I begin my month long journey of documenting my emotions concerning my impeding release. I have found that it isn't so much that I want to document the experience...I HAVE to. Writing has been my saving grace, my refuge, my place of safety...the one thing they haven't been able to take away from me and I am depending on the gift God gave to pull me through once more. With that being said; I am officially counting down.

"Pain is inevitable. Suffering is optional."

-M. Kathleen Casey

Fed Up

The officers' keys, dangling in my ears
Their constant threats and belligerent jeers
Their flashlights shining in my eyes
Every two hours, throughout the night
Orders are barked with no regard for humanity; no respect is in sight
The random, rambling, and ransacking of all of my belongings
Holding an ID and reciting a number; they have systematically branded me for life

The strip searches and interrogations
The constant stares of contempt
The intrusive censoring, of any mail that is sent
Legal today, contraband tomorrow
With every shift change, different rules follow

Sixty-eight and a wake, is how long I have to take
Living under condition; I have grown to hate
After five years and nine months
As a ward of the state

9

"The prisoner is not the one who has committed a crime, but the one who clings to his crime and lives it over and over."

-Henry Miller

30 Days and a Wake-Up   August 2nd, 2011

I sit in a bathroom stall writing this entry so that I don't disturb my roommates. Over the course of the last six years I have spent countless moments like this because at 1am…it's lights out. The rules of the institution say that it's time for me to go night-night but, I'm not ready so, I take advantage of one of the few loopholes found here to solve my dilemma. The security lights that always stay on have provided me hours to read and write once it's finally quiet.

Today, has been an all-day brainstorming session. My mind can't stop thinking of the dire situation some of these women will face upon their release back into a society in which they aren't equipped to live in. Most of them aren't prepared and will unfortunately find themselves in the revolving door of recidivism.

I attended my last "Pizza in the Park" event and it was emotional. The event isn't actually held in a park or outside. It was designed to be that way but the administration doesn't feel comfortable with the entire inmate population all in one place at one time…with good reason.

There are volunteers who have come into the institution faithfully and unselfishly gave of themselves to me the entire time I've been here and they have no idea how hard it is to say goodbye. My release will feel like the first day at a new school. I will have to develop relationships with new people who I can only hope will be the anchors I need to keep me grounded and most importantly…free.

The release list for September 1st came down today and I couldn't stop looking at it. Even, now it's hard to fathom that my name is on it. In October of 2005, September 2011 seemed to be an eternity away but, it's here now and I am so ready to spread my wings and fly…far, far, away from here.

On another note, today was one of those days when I was just ready for this to be over and I ask myself; 'When did I become so intolerant?' I had resigned within myself to be content throughout my entire sentence to take away the power of prison officials to break me. That acceptance turned out to be the reason why my journey in prison hasn't been as hard as other's have been. The minute you lose your self-control here -- you lose because prison is an obstacle course that wasn't designed for us to win so, when you give in to those impulses to live up to their notion that we are merely 'unruly animals', it's hard to get off of that path.

ANGER was the root cause of my bad attitude today and it was caused by...'HOT DOG BUNS'. I know it sounds crazy but, I will explain. When incarcerated you have to create your own happiness, your own reason to be excited; my elation has been stimulated by my favorite prison meal...hot dogs. It wasn't because it was tasty but, it is the only meal prepared here that reminds me of home because it was my favorite food there... I actually stopped looking at the menu so that I could be surprised when I heard someone announce that it was 'hot dog day'. A few people got a good laugh when they started to notice my reaction.

Today, I was excited; IT WAS HOT DOG DAY ONCE AGAIN! My excitement was short lived and I found myself perplexed because the makeshift yeast buns that I have become accustomed to, were replaced with 'real' hot dog buns. I sat at the table and haphazardly ripped the bun opened from the bottom because the buns I had become accustomed to were merely yeast buns made by inmates that weren't cut opened for our convenience. Evidently within the last six years, I have forgotten how they worked and it made me angry.

For the last six years, I psyched myself out of this whole experience so that I could survive. I thought that I was beating the system at their own game and that by doing so I would simply walk out of prison with my sanity intact. I became so entrenched in 'survival mode' that I never even realized how cunningly the system had ripped me away from reality. Now, I find myself terrified to discover what else I have forgotten how to do.

Six years is a relatively short amount of time in light of the 35 years a few of these women have served in prison but, to the real world—I have been gone for a long time and today I was faced with the realization that in 30 days I won't be in Kansas anymore. How will I cope?

"If you are going through hell, keep going."

-Winston Churchill

29 Days and a Wake-Up   August 3rd, 2011

Today, is Wednesday, the day that will be forever immortalized in my mind as 'The Infamous Inspection Day' and it started off crazy as usual. Every Wednesday morning before the sun could rise, I have performed the ritual of stripping my bed of its covers so that they could be laundered by the commissary. I can almost imagine my laundry piling up at home because I am waiting to hear someone yell, "Last call for laundry!" I'm starting to believe that I am going to suffer from Post-Traumatic Stress Disorder because the blinders are being lifted from my eyes and I now realize just how emotionally traumatic being incarcerated actually is. I have had to forget about my life as it was--- as I have been forced to adjust to being in prison. Now, I have to try to piece together the shattered remnants of a past life that I have a difficult time remembering. Am I really ready for what awaits me on the other side of these walls?

"Your life is still unwritten. You can still find your true self."

-Oprah Winfrey

Uncertainty and Assurance

I don't know why, life's storms roll in and threaten to overtake me
Why the rain of pain pours down so hard, that at times I can barely see
But, I know Who has the ability to save, what satan attempts to devour
I don't know what tomorrow holds but; I know Who holds tomorrow.

I don't know why, there are times I feel, I don't have the strength to
face another day
Times when I'm, afraid to go on, because I can't seem to find my way
But, I know, Who can replace my weakness and fears;
with courage and fill me with power
I don't know what tomorrow holds but; I know Who holds tomorrow.

I don't know why someone so full of life, is gone in the blink of an eye
Despite my best efforts to understand; I will never completely know why
But, I know Who can take something as ugly as death; and make it as
beautiful, as the rarest flower
I don't know what tomorrow holds but; I know Who holds tomorrow.

I don't know why moments of unbearable pain,
has to reach the depths of my soul
Bringing with them, emotions and tears,
I am unable to conceal or control
But, I know Who understands,
and will soothe my deepest sorrows
I don't know what tomorrow holds but; I know Who holds tomorrow.

I can't grasp the meaning of so many things;
they all remain mysteries
But, I don't need answers as long as God stands right beside me.
I can be victorious and never have to be a coward because,
I don't know what tomorrow holds but; I know Who holds tomorrow

"We turn to God for help when our foundations are shaking, only to learn that it is God Who is shaking them."

-Charles C. West

28 Days and a Wake-Up   August 4th, 2011

I had the day off from my job as G.E.D. Level English/Essay Writing Tutor because some of my students were taking the GED test. It makes me so happy to know that I have played a part in someone's success after the gigantic scarlet letter 'P' (for prison) has been forever etched in my life's history; so called proof that I am a menace to society… which is a totally false statement about me but, it is what most of America believes about returning citizens.

Other than nail biting, I have never had any other nervous habits but, with each passing day, the closer I get to September 1st, the chronic itching I have developed is progressively getting worse. My face is acne-central and up to this point, I was spared this horrible skin condition- even through puberty but now it's on and popping…literally and I am frustrated. I scrutinize every blemish, every pound I have gained in the last 6 months, my mannerisms, and the list could go on and on of the things I think will make me automatically stand out as a 'convict'. Paranoia 101 is an automatic prerequisite for prison; I guess I am a late enrollee. Go figure.

"Three hundred years ago a prisoner condemned to the Tower of London, carved on the wall of his cell this sentiment to keep up his spirits during his long imprisonment: 'It is not adversity that kills, but the impatience with which we bear adversity.'

-James Keller

Victimized

Her fingers are inside my collar
I feel her touching my neck
Unfamiliar hands move over my chest
I hold my breath, as she makes
Her way over, then under my breasts…
Something's different this time.

I close my eyes because others are watching
I'm humiliated and filled with shame
As spectators are allowed to watch me
Be violated, once again.

She moves slowly, across my abdomen
Then completely, around my waist
She's on one knee
As her hands now slide
Down the outside, of each of my legs.

Back up over, my inner thighs
She grazes my secret place
I refuse to allow, one tear to fall
As I feel myself, wanting to cry.

Instead I look my captor in the eyes
But she will never understand
What it's like for me
To lay down tonight
And be haunted by a stranger's hand.

"At the moment when the road looks the harshest, and you think you cannot continue on that is when you relearn your first mode of transportation; you crawl. You dig your fingers into the dirt, and propel yourself forward with your toes, but you never give up. You've gotta learn to bend with the sway. You never know what is around the next curve."

- *Sai Marie Johnson*

27 Days and a Wake-Up   August 5th, 2011

Another uneventful day in SCDC. There was one soothing aspect of it; rain. A thunderstorm rolled in early this afternoon and it was like music to my ears. It was the perfect lullaby to set the mood for a well-deserved afternoon nap.

I went to the cafeteria twice today. That is significant because I stopped going three weeks ago. The officers loud yelling, the threat of cell restriction for simply 'looking like' you are talking and the inhumane time limit placed on eating, the corralling of us into and out of the cafeteria more like livestock as opposed to human beings just became too much…today I saw nothing had changed…like I really expected it to.

I received an Order to Report (a summons for inmates to be somewhere in the institution) today for Wednesday, August 10th for me to pick up my release papers; known here as pink papers. I am ready but nervous. I'm almost three weeks away from the door and I have no definite plans yet. I have to keep reminding myself that now is not the time to lose the faith that has been my lifeline throughout this ordeal.

What is Cell Restriction?

Cell Restriction is a form of punishment where inmates are made to wear vests that are color-coordinated to match the color assigned to their living quarters. The vests signify that an inmate is not allowed outside of their cell without permission. When on cell restriction, inmates aren't allowed to go outside for their rec period. They are also not allowed to use the telephone, go to the bathroom, or shower without an officer's permission. Cell Restriction can last from 24-72 hours. If an inmate is caught without their vest on or if they do any of the above mentioned things without permission, they can be sent to lock-up where they will probably lose more privileges.

"The man of virtue makes the difficulty to be overcome his first business, and success only a subsequent consideration."

-Confucius

26 Days and a Wake-Up   August 6th, 2011

Reluctantly, at the request of one of my fellow inmates I braved the cafeteria for brunch—entire experience sucked. I don't know how I would cope if I had to do any more time than I have. I could feel myself on the verge of becoming sick as I ate. It saddens me to think of all of the people who will have to endure this for life…and to think that there are people in society who support the death penalty. If they had the slightest idea of what prison is truly like; if they knew that prison is absolute psychological torture; if they knew that it is a living hell, would it quench their thirst for blood? If I had a life sentence, I would welcome death; I would practically beg for it rather than endure this forever. I know that there are lifers who have entertained the same idea but, somehow they have found the strength to keep fighting and live in spite of their circumstances. I will always admire them.

I signed up for church (yes, we have to sign up to attend worship services) *Redemption World Outreach Church* came tonight and they always manage to change the atmosphere when they minister. A former SCDC inmate spoke to us tonight. He is now the director of a transitional housing program. Seeing and hearing his story reminded me of what I have to do once I am released. God has gotten me through this so that I can help those who are coming after me and *I WILL **NOT** FORGET!*

"All misfortune is but a stepping stone to fortune."

-Henry David Thoreau

25 Days and a Wake-Up   August 7th, 2011

Another one for the record books! I'm another step closer to being free. I slept most of the day and now that I think about it, I have barely seen 15 minutes of daylight all weekend long. I've been denying it but, since I can be honest on paper, I will admit that I think I am experiencing some degree of depression right now. The anxiety is taking its toll on my body. I can't believe I've come this far to start cracking up at the end.

One thing I won't miss about prison is waiting for money and visits. Today, I was feeling really down in my spirit and I really hoped that my mom would come to visit me but, she didn't. Looking outside of myself and my wants I understand because $3.50 per gallon and she is probably buying my release clothes as I write this. Times are hard and from that perspective it helps me to not take the lack of visitation personally.

My roommate and I were talking today and we discussed several women here who have never had a visit. One woman is on her 12th year—she has been incarcerated since the age of 17 and has never once had a visit. Another woman has done 25 years and another 15 years—all without a single visit. These are the stories that have helped me get through prison. Anytime I started feeling sorry for myself, I would think about the stories lifers here have told me. I would look at them smiling whenever we were outside during our rec period—enjoying the measure of life they still have and suddenly, my problems didn't seem so bad. They changed my perception of life in general and in doing so…they saved mine.

"The greater the difficulty to be overcome, the more will it be seen to the glory of God how much can be done by prayer and faith."

-George Müller

April Nachelle Barksdale

Summertime: Past, Present, Future

Going back to the summer of '85
When I was nine years old and I was swinging high.
I was playing hopscotch, had an Easy Bake; was outside with my sister on our roller
skates.

I watched schoolhouse rock; I loved my Care Bear; had Jellies on my feet and colored
beads in my hair.
Red Light, Green Light was the game to play
Street lights came on, had to call it a day.

Twenty-five years later, it's summer again
Looking forward to the day when this madness ends
People running my life; got me wearing state clothes
Can't go outside because the yard is closed
Can't walk on the grass; better stay in line
Head back in the dorm because it's count time.

September 1st, 2011
Almost Labor Day and it will feel like Heaven
With all my stuff packed, pink papers in hand
I'll say my number one more time and goodbye to the man

I'll be free on my porch, sipping lemonade
Showing all of my friends that I learned to play Spades

I'll be back with my family and I'll be just fine
Enjoying my freedom and summertime.

"Success in the affairs of life often serves to hide one's abilities, whereas adversity frequently gives one an opportunity to discover them.

-Horace

24 Days and a Wake-Up   August 8th, 2011

Count is delayed—as usual. Today has been just another day in prison. The temperature was high so, the yard was closed which meant no afternoon rec.

This morning, I facilitated the *Creative Writing Workshop* that I started. I teach the only inmate led class in the prison and its surreal how even in prison I have been granted so much favor. I have been amazed to discover my natural talent and ability to teach. While teaching this class I am able to give others tools to help them liberate themselves and that in itself has been so rewarding. I pray that there will be opportunities outside of prison for me to continue teaching and empowering others.

Now that I am on this side of my sentence, I don't see or acknowledge the negative impact incarceration has had on me. There have been so many eye opening, aha moments of self-discovery that I choose to focus on the good that I will be taking with me.

Many of the other women being released and I have forged a bond. There are two days from everyone's prison experience that will be forever etched into our minds; the day we arrived and the day we leave. At this moment, I think we lean on each other for support and encouragement to make it across these last hurdles. We have bonded because we will reach the end of our journeys together. A friend who left prison three years ago has offered to send me release clothes and I am so emotional. Someone left here and cared enough to look back and help me out of the dungeon she was already freed from. Her gesture made me think of two things: 1. We—prisoners, ex-offenders, convicts…returning citizens are not all bad people. 2. Who will be the people that will need me to pay it forward for the blessings that I now receive?

"*Look not mournfully into the past, it comes not back again. Wisely improve the present, it is thine. Go forth to meet the shadowy future without fear and with a manly heart.*"

-Henry Wadsworth Longfellow

23 Days and a Wake-Up   August 9th, 2011

Slow but steady wins the race—that is what I have to keep reminding myself.

I attended my last birthday party in prison tonight. *The Birthday Club'* is a prison ministry that was started by an elderly couple from the area; he is 75, she is 72 and they have been having birthday parties for the women at Leath every month for the past 18 years! They started at McCormick Correctional Institution (men's prison) before they ever started coming here. It is so easy to fall into that trap of feeling as if you are forgotten here. Every day we are reminded that all that matters is the number we have been branded with and count clearing. I will never forget how these loving people gave of themselves and used their limited resources so unselfishly to make me and others feel special on our birthdays.

Tonight, I watched this show on television called, *Take the Money and Run'*. Two contestants are given a briefcase containing $100,000 and have one hour to hide it before they are apprehended by the staged law enforcement officials. Detectives then have 48 hours to try to find where they stashed it. If they find the money they get to keep it; if they don't the contestants do. After watching this show I was astounded by how easily I am able to think like a criminal now. I have never done drugs, sole or manufactured them but, I can talk about it now as if I have simply from having to listen to the war stories of some of my roommates after the lights went out.

I have realized that despite my best efforts; in some ways, I have become a product of my environment but, I refuse to become another recidivism statistic.
Martin Luther King, Jr said something that will always be the catalyst for the way I live my life. He said, "The time is always right, to do what is right."

"Being challenged in life is inevitable, being defeated is optional."
-Roger Crawford

Double Vision

*As I gaze into the magnificent blue sky; I notice it's filled with brilliant white clouds that
seem to be suspended in mid-air. I'm amazed that I never recognized the pure essence of
nature and the wondrous works of God until now…
That I'm honest with myself; I wonder if my attentiveness is genuine, or am I just
masking and disguising once again; not wanting to face the truth?*

*Could it be that I keep my head towards the sky, so that my eyes are averted from the
reality that surrounds me and glistens in the noonday sun—the razor wire that intrudes
upon the horizon o reiterate the magnitude of my circumstances; inadvertently preventing
me from seeing beyond these walls.*

*Is the sunset really that beautiful, or am I thinking deep in my heart, that if I stare into
the heavens long enough, God will acknowledge my silent but desperate cries for freedom.*

*Am I in awe of the moon in the star-filled sky or; am I inwardly wishing that the
darkness of the night would overtake me and end my misery?*

*Is that prick I feel in my heart each time I see a sparrow take flight because I am
enveloped with joy over another one of god's creations or; is that sensation merely a twinge
of envy because that little bird's solo flight is a subtle reminder to me of what it was once
like to be free?*

"Little minds are tamed and subdued by misfortune, but great minds rise above them."

-Washington Irving

22 Days and a Wake-Up   August 10th, 2011

Oh boy, I'm feeling really official now—I received my release papers today! YAAAYYY!!! I know that the show isn't over until the fat lady sings but, I swear I can almost hear her warming up.

In the midst of my elation, during our release orientation the harsh reality of prison sucked the joy completely out of me. The staff member who conducted our orientation told us we couldn't wear flip flops when we left. An older woman asked about sandals—the staff member asked what type of sandals. The inmate replied, "Birkenstocks." And the staff member said, "Look, I don't even know what those are. I am just a poor, working class, state employee barely making it because you all get all of my money." It was the first of many cheap shots she took at us today and it was a reminder to me of just how I became so bitter towards the system I once had so much respect for; despite only being a number to them. Her comments reminded me of what I will have to face when dealing with some people in society. Today, I was more motivated to never return to this place again.

"A setback is a set-up for a comeback"

-Bishop T.D. Jakes

21 Days and a Wake-Up   August 11th, 2011

I went to my *One-on-One* Bible Study with Mrs. Moore today and I am always in awe of the commitment the volunteers have to being a positive part of our lives.

I spent the rest of the day organizing my Creative Writing lesson for the next week and while I was in the Chaplain's Area, I was given a spur of the moment interview with the transitional program I hope to be accepted into. At 4 pm I arrived to my interview hopeful, only to have my faith shaken to the core by the revelation that was made. I have been by prison standards a 'model inmate' for almost 6 years—not perfect by any means but, I haven't been a troublemaker and I haven't given the staff any trouble. On numerous occasions I have been looked down upon because I have vehemently expressed my disdain about things here that I considered to be wrong. I have stood up for myself and made enemies in the process.

To make a long story short, one staff member in particular has been my arch enemy and I still haven't pinpointed exactly why and today her issues with me threaten my chances of being accepted into this particular program. How sad that this person placed here to help us has been my greatest hindrance. The lesson I am learning in all of this is to trust God, but it's a reminder of why I must not let my story go untold. My story isn't unique; there are others whose voices have been silenced by fear and by the administrations unwillingness to allow us the due process we are entitled to.

"Our very survival depends on our ability to stay awake, to adjust to new ideas, to remain vigilant and to face the challenge of change."
-Martin Luther King Jr.

The Making of a Fighter

The hurt you caused hasn't hindered me from attempting to accomplish my dreams.
The sadness you caused, hasn't made me surrender, although that's the way it might seem.

I was bruised but not broken, by the things you did to me.
I was weak but now I'm strong; frustrated but not yet defeated.

I'm too blessed to be stressed, over all of the things, I've been forced to leave behind.
The race isn't over because, I've caught, a glimpse of the finish line.

I'm too persistent to be persuaded, by your schemes of yesterday.
I'm too determined to be denied, the awards that await me ahead.

Every tear that I cried, made me strive to achieve my goals and move higher.
Now, instead of hating, I thank you; for helping to make me a fighter.

"Times of great calamity and confusion have ever been productive of the greatest minds. The purest ore is produced from the hottest furnace, and the brightest thunderbolt is elicited from the darkest storm."

-Charles Caleb Colson

20 Days and a Wake-Up   August 12th, 2011

No work today and I enjoyed my day off. My headaches are becoming more frequent and I know it's due to tension and stress.

I received an acceptance letter from a transitional program today. The information I received has peaked my interest so, I am writing back for more details.

This whole process of being released has been very though provoking. I consider myself to be resourceful person. I started my search for housing or placement into a transitional program in June and less than three weeks away from maxing out and nothing is etched in stone yet. I spend a lot of time thinking about the people who don't know what to do and those who don't have any place to go. What will they do? I have a definite alternative should need to go that route. This whole release procedure has been a joke and I really see clearly why South Carolina and the nation have problems with recidivism. Many of the women being released with me are not prepared for re-entry into society and the bus ticket the state is giving them on September 1st should be round trip because the South Carolina Department of Corrections has failed to do their job of rehabilitating them and according to statistics; 75% of us will return.

"In the midst of winter, I found there was within me an invincible summer."

-Albert Careb

April Nachelle Barksdale

Haiku

Free but still not free

Life in prison is pure hell

How did I get here?

"Life's challenges are not supposed to paralyze you, they're supposed to help you discover who you are."
-Bernice Johnson Reagon

19 Days and a Wake-Up   August 13th, 2011

Another lazy day. I spent half of it in bed trying to shake this persistent headache and I worked on my resume.

I can hardly believe that it is really winding down and I find myself apprehensive and excited. A woman named Lisa Rogers who was a volunteer here at one time wrote to me today and offered to assist me with clothing and personal hygiene products. She even said that she would help me with furniture when I got into my own place. Lisa was a great mentor with Prison Fellowship who has been such a great help to me during my incarceration. Her selfless devotion and commitment to those of us here in prison gives me hope. My only hope is that I can one day give others the same thing that these people have given to me.

"Surmounted difficulties not only teach, but hearten us in our future struggles."

-James Sharpe

18 Days and a Wake-Up   August 14th[th], 2011

Another day closer to going home and I find myself longing for the simple things like lying in bed watching TV, being able to get a cold drink in the middle of the night and walk outside barefooted. I am so ready to just hold my children and have the ability to talk to them anytime that I want to.

The weekends in prison can be very depressing because we only get one hour and 15 minutes outside per day. Daylight Savings Time was pure torture for me throughout my incarceration because the sun was still shining until almost 9 pm and I was locked inside as early as 4 pm. I wonder if people know what these types of things does to a person's mental state.

LIFE--- I can hardly wait to live again.

"When it is dark enough, you can see the stars."

-Ralph Waldo Emerson

17 Days and a Wake-Up   August 15th, 2011

TODAY IS MY 35TH BIRTHDAY...the last one I will spend in prison. Prison is always perceived as this intolerable place full of volatile, angry, and uncompassionate people but, I have had more memorable and joyous birthdays while incarcerated than I ever had 'on the streets' which says a lot about my life before prison.

I woke up this morning to balloons on my locker (made from paper of course) given to me by my roommate Savannah. One of the most notorious women here...according to society—Susan Smith; once again made sure that I knew she was thinking of me on my birthday by sending me a card that she made. A lot of people outside of these walls won't understand this but, she has become a great friend to me.

I was treated to a birthday dinner of beef tips in gravy, macaroni and cheese, fried rice, and pinto beans...yes we make a way out of no way in prison.

I had a great day. My best friend Zandra and I spent our afternoon rec period together and she made me dinner too!!! Fried rice, BBQ ham, Mac and cheese and a brownie that tasted like it was made at home. She cried in and off the entire time and it made me sad because I have been on the side she is on now and I know how hard it is when someone you're close to leaves. In the end you eventually find a way to cope because at the end of the day it's simply a part of surviving prison.

Side Note:
The thoughtful dinners made for me today were against the rules in prison.

"Getting over a painful experience is much like crossing monkey bars. You have to let go at some point in order to move forward."

-C.S. Lewis

The Stranger Within

Who am I?

Who is she; the woman in the mirror, staring back at me?

Where is the woman, who was once plagued with pain;

Who was hidden beneath guilt and covered in shame?

Where is the woman, who once hated me; the once who was always unsure, of who and what she could be?

Where is the woman who never knew her worth or; understood her destiny?

Where is the woman who never felt loved?

She is I.

And I am she.

I'm the woman who now adores everything about me.

"Sometimes in tragedy we find life's purpose—the eye sheds a tear to find its focus."

-Robert Brault

16 Days and a Wake-Up   August 16th, 2011

Today, I had the chance to give back…It was my roommate Savannah's birthday! She was excited about her paper birthday balloons and the gifts she received from all of her friends. I also made decorations for someone else whose birthday was also today after she didn't receive anything and it made her day.

We received our 'Captain D's' fish plates today. No matter how many times I have ordered food during the I.R.C. (Inmate Representative Committee) projects, I am always left unfulfilled because…it is never quite like home.

I received mail from my children today for the first time in 11 months. Enclosed was a picture of them with their dad and I stared at it mesmerized because it was the first time I had laid eyes on them in 30 months. My ex-husband wrote a short letter and I wonder if he knows that keeping my children away from me was one of the cruelest things he has ever done to me and despite my deep relationship with God; I am finding hard to forgive and forget.

The birthday cards from my children really brightened my day and I couldn't stop crying.

It's almost over; that is all I keep telling myself but…this seems like the longest month of my life.

"If you don't like something change it; if you can't change it, change the way you think about it."
-Mary Engelbreit

15 Days and a Wake-Up   August 17th, 2011

Another day in prison…another inspection day…etc. etc. etc. It's hard for me to remain motivated because I am just so ready to go.

I went to my hair care appointment today and I cut my hair for the last time in prison. That process was so bittersweet because it was in the prison beauty salon that I met so many people, lifted so many spirits, and discovered my God-given talent for styling hair. Being in the salon was like being in my very own oasis because it was away from the general area. I watched so many sunrises and sunsets from the salon window and it was where I received my greatest hope of freedom because it was the only view in the prison where the horizon wasn't intruded upon by that glistening razor wire that was a constant reminder that I was indeed in prison. I am so very grateful that God placed me in so many positions that provided me with various degrees of freedom that helped me make it through some of my darkest days here. He is faithful.

"All great changes are preceded by chaos."
-Deepak Chopra

You

Rejected, betrayed, criticized, despised; insulted, humiliated, and then crucified;
Yet not once did You complain.
You knew by losing Your very own life; everything is what I would gain.
I repaid You by living in sin and, using Your name in vain.

I stand before You unworthy of, the mercy You so freely give.
Despite the many times I failed; You continue to love me still.

You faithfully carry each and every burden, which I am unable to bear.
I've doubted and turned my back on You but, for me You have always cared.

You bestow life and countless blessings upon me; though I only deserve curses and death.
All of the times I walked away from You; my side You never left.

Thinking of all of the things You have done and endured just for me.
I'm left speechless; there are no words I can say.
I can only drop down to my knees to worship and praise Your magnificent name; to give
honor to the Friend I never knew.

Jesus, You've given so much to me; now I'm giving my all back to You.

"A man should never be ashamed to own he has been wrong, which is but saying, in other words, that he is wiser today than he was yesterday."

-Alexander Pope

14 Days and a Wake-Up   August 18ᵗʰ, 2011

Prison doesn't change from day to day. It's like waking up in a real life version of the Bill Murray movie, *'Groundhog Day'*. Every day is a rerun of the previous day and tomorrow will be the same…redundant. I suppose that is why I could never stay committed to keeping a journal since I have been here—writing the same thing over and over again becomes depressing after a while. Being in prison, you learn to live in denial about the reality of the situation you are in. In your mind you pretend that the real world doesn't exist and that PRISON is all that there is.

It has been while writing these daily entries into this journal that I discovered that I have grown accustomed to living in denial—it has been and is the only way to survive this ordeal and leave with your sanity. Maybe not so much just denial but, it is whatever helps you make it through the days, months, and years that pass by.

Oh, how could I forget to mention that today I was begrudgingly given 2 of the mandatory 7 rolls of toilet paper we are issued every month…another sign that it is almost over. How am I ever going to regroup out there when everything… even down to toilet paper has been provided and regulated for 6 years?

"Adversity precedes growth."

-Rosemarie Rosetti

13 Days and a Wake-Up   August 19th, 2011

I spent my day off from work in excruciating pain caused by my arthritis. Days like this make me even more eager to go home because the medical personnel in this prison could care less about our overall well-being.

I slept some and read some—I don't read fiction…except for James Patterson and his books have helped me endure some of my longest days and nights because they are intriguing and somehow have the ability to snatch me out of this living nightmare I am in; if only for a moment.

I had a telephone interview with another transitional program and received a copy of their rules and regulations which seem to be a lot like prison and I am not sure that I want to or can deal with that.

I mailed a letter to my mom today asking her if it was okay for me to change my plans and just go to her house; hopefully she says yes. I can't believe and never imagined that I would be 35 years old, moving back in with my mom but, here I am and it is not a good feeling at all. I pray that stark reminder will be my motivation to move quickly towards independence.

"Courage comes from clinging to a hand infinitely larger than your own."

-Unknown

The Deepest Part of Me

My past haunts me every day.
I'm constantly looking over my shoulder
Running from demons no one else can see
Unless they enter the deepest part of me.

Whenever a sudden movement is made; I'm searching for somewhere to hide.
Whenever a voice is raised; I fight hard not to cry.
Whenever I'm given a compliment; I long to see what they see.
That reflection of myself is hidden within, the deepest part of me.

I make myself up and try to smile; hoping to disguise my life's history.
Wondering which of the people I meet, aren't blind and can really see
The lack of confidence and low self-esteem in the deepest part of me.

I try to convince myself I'm beautiful and there's nothing I can't achieve
Then those voices creep back in saying, "Don't you remember me?"
They say, "You're stupid! You're pathetic! You're nothing!"
And that's what I believe because, those are the words that have been etched and are
rooted in the deepest part of me.

When you stare into my eyes, do you see the person who's dying to be free?
The person who desires, and longs to be loved, for all of eternity.
Will you take time, to find the person inside, of the deepest part of me?

"Ambition is the path to success. Persistence is the vehicle you arrive in."

-Bill Bradley

12 Days and a Wake-Up   August 20th, 2011

September 1st...PLEASE HURRY---I feel as if I am losing my mind! These people; inmates and staff alike are hard to tolerate right now. The disrespect, the pettiness, and constant bickering is almost too much.

The highlight of my day was being able to talk to my sister Cha'Ron, my niece Jessica and my great-niece Mimie. I call them my instant family because my sister found out about me and we 'met' so to speak since my incarceration. It's amazing that God is already restoring what was taken away even before I leave prison and I am grateful.

I was hoping I would get a visit today but, no such luck. I just find myself longing and aching for freedom.

"Every setback might be the thing that makes you carry on and fight all the harder and become that much better."

-Les Paul

Reflections during a Storm

Raindrops are falling from the sky
Like my life at times, I wonder why
Each drop reminds me of tears I have cried
And the childhood dreams I allowed to die
The countless opportunities I let pass me by…
And the rain just keeps on falling.

With each clap of thunder, my heart still breaks
As I remember advice I refused to take
Anxious to grow up, I didn't want to wait
I tried to change things but, it was just too late
Now, I sit in a place, from which I can't escape…
And the rain just keeps on falling

When lightning flashes in my mind
I think of days, when the sun still shined
And all of the things I left behind
To search for the love I was determined to find
Only to discover, that it was a waste of time…
And the rain just keeps on falling.

With each gust of wind, each step, takes more effort than the last
The riverbed of my life is filling fast
I'm tormented by regrets and circumstances from my past
As I drown in despair, fighting for my life, seems like a useless task…
And the rain just keeps on falling.

A man adapts himself to circumstances as water shapes itself to the vessel that contains it.

-Chinese Proverb

11 Days and a Wake-Up   August 21st, 2011

OMG!!! Today, a woman gave birth to a baby girl in lock-up!!! This is way too much! Once again an incident of blatant negligence on the part of prison officials and no one will lose their job because of it.

Inmate.com --- the name we have given the rumor mill here in prison, says that this woman screamed all day today and her pleas for help were ignored. Nothing new about that!

So many questions about what actually happened and no answers--- only speculation. The sweep it under the rug policy is in full effect but, what remains is that we are regarded as less than human beings here in all ways. This woman had a baby; and life threatening illnesses or medical concerns are oftentimes always ignored. Moments like the birth of this child today...within the confines of a prison, reminds me that if God allows me to walk out of those gates on September 1st...I am indeed a lucky woman because some of us leave in body bags.

"Start where you are. Use what you have. Do what you can."

-Arthur Ashe

Imprisoned Rage

Every day that I'm in this place, rage gradually consumes me.
I'm unable to express how I feel.
I want to hit someone or something.
Damn!!! I just want to scream; to somehow release this consuming rage
That's growing inside of me.

Angry, agitated, pissed off aggravated
By the system designed
To break me down
To the least common
Denominator of me

Hatred, jealousy, envy, and deceit
Is all that now surrounds me
Demons disguised as people
Are trapped inside; the prisons they've built in their minds
They don't expect me to fight
But, to simply accept the status quo
To become a part, of their twisted plot
Where condemned women, are merely pawns
In a game they will never win

Please help me!
I'm going insane!
I just can't take anymore.
This rage is consuming me.
I'm barely alive because I'm dying inside; for someone to let me out
I'm crying but no one hears, the sound of my lonely tears

I wonder which of the breaths I struggle to take will be my last
This rage rumbles like a volcano ready to erupt; spewing untamed emotions
I try to hold on, to the smallest part of who I used to be
As I become more and more like the animals around me; a product of my environment

As I sit alone, my circumstances, add fuel to the inferno of rage
That is slowly destined to be, the eventual death of me.

A gem cannot be polished without friction, nor can man be perfected without trials.

-Danish Proverb

10 Days and a Wake-Up   August 22nd, 2011

Everywhere I went today, all I heard about was, 'Leath's First Baby'. There is a lot of excitement; especially form the lifers and some of the women who have been incarcerated since they were teenagers. They were mesmerized at the sight of an officer holding a new life when imminent death is the only thing that has been their reality. There are others who have been traumatized by this incident because they realize that the system is more likely than not, broken beyond repair and that this poor woman's plight could in all actuality become our own.

When we are treated in this manner I wonder if they ever stop to consider that the theory of *'Six Degrees of Separation'* could be playing out before their very eyes. If they did, maybe their attitudes and ill treatment towards inmates would end because, then they would realize---our destinies aren't that far away from being their own.

"A bend in the road is not the end of the road...unless you fail to make the turn."

-Unknown

9 Days and a Wake-Up   August 23rd, 2011

Well, it looks like all of the action is taking place at the end of my sentence. Today, I experienced my first earthquake! I was in the computer room in education when I thought that I was having another vertigo episode until I turned around and saw file cabinets and a cart rocking back and forth. Everyone didn't feel it; only one person I was working with didn't think I was crazy. The nightly news confirmed what I already knew. A 5.8 earthquake struck in Virginia and even damaged the Washington Monument in D.C. It was the strongest earthquake we have had on the East coast since 1897.

Now, there is a hurricane brewing in the Atlantic that is threatening to hit the U.S. this weekend. One thing about prison that is reassuring to those of us here is that we are probably in a safer position than anyone in the state at the moment. Prison officials go above and beyond to make sure that we are all safe…in other words; 'accounted for'.

Outside of those things, my day has been uneventful. I had fun with my co-workers and realized that I am really going to miss them when I leave.

"We who live in prison, and in whose lives there is no event but sorrow, have to measure time by throbs of pain, and the record of bitter moments."

-Unknown

838 Days

I haven't taken a bath or walked barefoot in the grass.
I haven't made love and I haven't been dancing...
In 838 days.

I haven't combed my children's hair, told them good morning, or kissed them good night.
I haven't helped them celebrate their birthdays...
In 838 days.

I haven't had a job, filed takes, used a computer, or voted in an election,
Laid eyes on the ocean, or been to the movies...
In 838 days.

I haven't driven a car, touched a dollar bill, or played with my kids at the park,
No P.T.A. meetings, no report cards, no help with projects or homework...
In 838 days.

I haven't pumped gas, washed a dish or washed a dish, or made a wish — upon a star
Because I haven't been allowed, outside at night...
In 838 days.

No Super Bowl parties, no internet access, no cooking the holiday meals
No decorating the Christmas tree
No zippers, buttons, jeans, or heels...
In 838 days.

I haven't been alone.
I haven't answered a phone.
I can't believe the things I took for granted and all of the things I've missed...
In 838 days.

"When the Japanese mend broken objects, they aggrandize the damage by filling the cracks with gold. They believe that when something's suffered damage and has a history it becomes more beautiful."

-Barbara Bloom

8 Days and a Wake-Up   August 24th, 2011

Downside…inspection day. Highlight…I received my release clothes today!!! My mom did a good job picking things out. Having on REAL CLOTHES felt like I was in a dream; I couldn't stop staring at myself in the mirror. I have a dressy t-shirt, some dark colored stretch jeans, and a pair of black, sling back, peep toe heels. God be with me in those shoes but, I want to start where I left off. I was surprised that I effortlessly fit into my size 12 jeans with room to spare. After elastic and only small, medium, and large options for so long, it felt so strange to handle a zipper and to be without my prison ID for the first time in six years.

I still wavering between going to my mom's or into a transitional program. Both choices have their own unique sets of pros and cons; I just have to keep praying for clarity.

Seven day countdown!!! One more inspection day and I am DONE!!!

"We must embrace pain and burn it as fuel for our journey."

-Kenji Miyazawa

7 Days and a Wake-Up   August 25th, 2011

Today, was my last Thursday in prison. I was accepted into the transitional program that I really wanted to get into only to have the rug ripped out from underneath me as I realized that I probably won't go there. Such a disappointment. Along with my acceptance letter was a list of program rules; one of which stated that I cannot visit with my family for two weeks after my release.—this includes my children. How will I ever be able to justify making a voluntary decision that prohibits me from seeing them after I have been gone for six years? I can't and won't do that to them. I just have to trust God to keep and guide me on my journey of uncertainty.

My One-on-One mentor didn't come today and I hate that I won't be able to say goodbye. The other volunteers brought in fruit today and it was SOOOO DELICIOUS!!! God gave me a taste of what's to come to ease my anxiety and what a blessing it was!

"Life consists not in holding good cards, but playing those you hold well.

\- **Josh Billings**

Questions Behind These Walls

How could they say no after I've done so much time, and made a change for the better?
Why didn't they see, my true remorse?
Did they even read my letters?
How do I endure this, for another year?
When this place that's responsible for "rehabilitating me"
Is slowly breeding anger, hatred and fears?

Will I spend the rest of my life trying to outlive my past?
Do I have the strength to go on?
Does my heart have the vibrancy to last?
How do I hold on to, my deep desire for growth;
When they-they system
Tries so hard, to keep my self-esteem low?

How do I remain compassionate, when I'm forced to conceal,
My feelings and humanity, just to survive this ordeal?
Why should I continue to hope in brighter tomorrows when it slips through my fingers
like the sand of time; and its false promises create so much sorrow?

Why should my family stand by me, after I have been gone so long?
Is my expecting them to being selfish; or is it plain wrong?
How do I deal with the fact that my child says sometimes, she can't remember my face?
How do I remain positive in such a negative place?

How do I keep breathing when the weight of this trial is crushing the life out of me?
How do I look forward to the end when it's so very hard to see?
Why keep pleading for mercy when it seems like my prayers don't go any farther than the ceiling?
How can I not keep dreaming?
I've come too far not too.
How can God expect me to keep believing, when He continuously fails to come through?
How do I find answers to my questions when I don't have a clue how to?

"Adversity is like a strong wind. It tears away from us all but the things that cannot be torn, so that we see ourselves as we really are."

-Arthur Golden, Memoirs of a Geisha

6 Days and a Wake-Up   August 26th, 2011

No work scheduled for today but, I was still in education streamlining the English and essay writing of the G.E.D. classes into the format that I developed. How cool is it that? My style and method of teaching has been so effective, that the person over the Education Department here in the prison wants all of the English tutors to follow my plans.

This is just another example of how I have flourished during my incarceration. I was the lead stylist in the hair salon, I coordinated religious activities for various denominations when I worked in the Chaplains area, I was elected as the Inmate Representative Committee member for my living unit, I was a member of Operation Behind Bars (A program that gave people going through the court system a tour of prisons and an opportunity to hear inmate stories in an attempt to deter them from doing something to enter prison themselves) I rose from choir member to choir director, successfully completed the Electrical Wiring Class to become a Certified Electrical Apprentice. I facilitated the only inmate led class here and participated in a host of other activities that helped me grow as a person.

Prison hasn't been easy and is in no way something I am proud of but, I am thankful for the opportunity I have had to grow. I see others who haven't taken advantage of the opportunities here and it saddens me how the system continues to fail people. No prison officials or administration ever suggested that I become involved in any of the things that I did since I have been here. I made a decision to grow where I was planted and I wanted to have something positive to show for the six years of my life that I have been missing from society.

So, many people arrive to prison with nothing and leave the same way. It hurts me so much to see people leave and return over and over again because I know in my heart that no one wants to be in prison. I have come to understand that sometimes it's easier to be here than fight with nothing on the outside. God, give me the strength to find and lead the way upon my release.

"Everything that happens to us leaves some trace behind; everything contributes imperceptibly to make us what we are."

-Johann Wolfgang von Goethe

Submit to Authority?

Submit to authority… that's easier said than done
When I'm forced to comply simply because
They have the bullets and the guns?

Submit to authority…
And give R-E-S-P-E-C-T…
When there is no reciprocity, if you have six digits like me?

Submit to authority…
And tell the truth… so that they call me a liar
And send me to SMU?

Submit to authority…
When there is no chain of command…
When they are the judge, jury, and executioner
In this corrupted land?

Submit to authority…
That's difficult for me…
When they are allowed to degrade, humiliate
And sexually harass me?

Submit to authority…
And stand for what's right…
Only to be told, that because you're an inmate,
No one is concerned with your plight?

Submitting to authority in prison means…
Not ever saying what's on your mind
Allow the administration to mistreat you
Don't buck the system and everything will be just fine.

Submitting to authority…
Is hard to see…
When those in charge are obvious enemies.
We fight for our release
And they do all they can so that we can't be free.

Submit to authority…
And put on a show…
So that when outsiders come in…
They will never know that…

Submitting to authority…
Breeds anger and strife…
When they disregard an inmate's health, merely because she has "LIFE"
That's not worth saving to them?

Submit to authority…
I can't—not completely…
Not as long as there is no justice
No honor or integrity.

Submitting to authority…
I once believed that was the way
Until I saw what really goes on…
From this side of the gates.

"Loss makes artists out of us all as we weave new patterns in the fabric of our lives."

-Unknown

5 Days and a Wake-Up   August 23rd, 2011

I attended my last *Kairos Reunion* here in prison. Despite the personal battles I have faced as I anxiously wait to be released, I have managed to keep it together emotionally on the exterior; today that ended. As I stood before a gym full of inmates, many of whom have touched my life in their own unique way and before a lot of volunteers who have sacrificed of themselves to visit us here in prison… every month for six years! I cried. I cried because it finally hit me that I am leaving this place and returning to freedom. The relationships I forged here will be no more and I am sad and elated at the same time.

I gave a farewell speech about what *Kairos* has meant to me during my incarceration. I will never find words that can adequately describe the enormous impact *Kairos* had on my life. *Kairos* is the prison ministry organization that opened the doors to my heart and freed me from my own personal prison so, that I could develop an enduring relationship with God that kept me in perfect peace while I have been here in prison. What an amazing and priceless gift. I am confident that what *Kairos* gave to me will keep me as I walk out prison.

'They'll Know We Are Christians by Our Love'

Kairos means: 'God's Special Time'

"Man is not imprisoned by habit. Great changes in him can be wrought by crisis- once that crisis can be recognized and understood."

-Unknown

4 Days and a Wake-Up   August 28th, 2011

Another day closer to freedom. I don't have batteries for my radio because I haven't received money into my account so, that avenue of escape isn't available. No batteries also means no television which sucks. The T.V.'s don't play through their speakers; the channels have to be listened to through radio frequencies. I was fortunate enough to have been able to purchase a radio. Some people aren't and that means if they can't find someone willing to share; no television for them. Up until this moment, I never even thought about how weird it is going to be to actually hear a T.V. out loud after listening through earbuds for so long. Every day, I become more aware of just how much I will have to adjust to once I leave prison.

I have slept more over the last month than I have the entire time I have been incarcerated. If I am asleep I don't have to deal with the anxiety and the harsh reality that not everyone is happy to see people leave prison. There are women here who have been known to instigate fights with people scheduled for release. I have also seen people who were one day away from leaving, fall into the traps set for them and watched them lose their release day. I haven't made any enemies here but, I'm choosing to fly under the radar just to be on the safe side.

A personal thank you to **HIS Radio 89.3** in Greenville, SC. Your station was my lifeline so many days and night. Your encouragement and love of Christ permeated those prison walls and ministered directly to my heart when I needed it most.

"Nothing is better for self-esteem than survival."

-Martha Gellhorn

3 Days and a Wake-Up   August 29th, 2011

Today, I facilitated my last Creative Writing Class and it was bittersweet. My students and I had a lot of fun together and as much as I hate that it is over, I am overwhelmed by the possibilities that freedom may hold. The ladies were happy and proud to receive their certificates of completion and the compilation books I made of work they have done during the course of our 8 week workshop; little things mean a lot and excite us here.

My 'caseworker' if you can call her that, signed my release papers today. She has been paid to do absolutely nothing on my behalf over the last 6 years and today was no different. I signed in. She signed the papers and dryly said, "Good luck.", and before I could cross the threshold of her office door, she was screaming, "Next!"

We didn't have our afternoon rec period and they didn't even feel the need to give us an explanation as to why; another reason to stay out of prison. Here I am, a 35 year old woman and I am have to have permission to do something as simple as walk outside. Reality has a way of swiftly kicking you in the behind. I have wondered if my sudden heightened sensitivity and disdain for everything in this prison is God's way of giving me a reason to fight to never return to this place ever again. Needless to say…it's working.

"The purpose of life is the lesson."

- Shannon L. Alder

2 Days and a Wake-Up   August 30th, 2011

I am amazed at how well I have become at mentally taking myself out of 'prison'. I do it so well that there is a part of myself that yearns for freedom but, the defense mechanisms I have developed since being incarcerated to protect me from hurt, disappointments, and things that are out of my control, prevents me from expressing any genuine excitement until the gate is opened for me to walk through.

I started packing today and I felt a twinge of excitement but, I immediately turned it off—anything can happen in prison. Sometimes in prison it seems as if you can't win for losing and at times I have felt like I was Charlie Brown on his impossible quest to kick the football that Lucy constantly snatches away. My lack of enthusiasm is because, not only am I leaving this place, I am also leaving people I have come to care about behind. I feel that expressing my happiness is like slapping my roommate in the face because she has 9 years remaining on her 20 year sentence; enough time to do my sentence one and a half more times. I can't even wrap my heart and mind around that concept.

I can't believe all of the paper I have accumulated over the past 6 years but, then again I can because writing has truly been my saving grace.

Today, was the last day I will have to push a slip of paper through a screen and swipe an ID card to shop. I just realized that it has been six years since I have touched any money. WOW!

I went to rec with my friend Zandra who cried the entire time and it broke my heart; prison rules that prohibit touching prevented me from even hugging her. Talk about conflicting emotions. I feel so bad for her because I have been where she is but, today the elation that is finally building in my heart because of my impending date with freedom wouldn't allow me to cry with her and I felt like a cold-hearted animal. It's crazy that prison; the place I have come to despise, is also the place that I have so many fond memories of. It took me coming to prison to find myself. God, please help me find some sense of balance and give me the words to say as I write my goodbye letters tomorrow.

I glanced through my photo album today to show my roommate Savannah a picture of the kids and for the first time in 6 years—I smiled when I looked at them. I can't believe that I am so close to being reunited with my babies; who were 10, 8, and 5 when this nightmare began. They are now—16, 14, and 11.

"When the frustration of my helplessness seemed greatest, I discovered God's grace was more than sufficient. And after my imprisonment, I could look back and see how God used my powerlessness for His purpose. What He has chosen for my most significant witness was not my triumphs or victories, but my defeat."

-Charles Caleb Colton

1 Day and a Wake-Up   August 31st, 2011

I finished getting all of my things packed and I am done writing all of my letters. I cannot sleep and I am sure that I won't. I am thinking of the countless times I have laid awake at night wondering what it would feel like when it was my turn to leave. I remember the times I dreamt that I was free and at home with my family, only to be tortured by waking up in the same place…and crying because I was so sick and tired of doing time. I think of all of the moments I missed with my children, and it hurts me more than anyone will ever know.

After tomorrow I will never be forced to walk in a straight line. I will be able to choose what I want to eat. I can go for a walk anytime that I want. I will never be counted again. I will never hear, "Lights out!" I will wear a color other than tan. I can eat my meals at a normal pace and use real silverware (I was issued an orange plastic spork and cup engraved with my name and SCDC# the day I entered prison). I can see my children every day without having to be strip searched afterwards. I can have more than ten books. I will get paid for working. I can look at the sun rise and set without razor wire tainting the horizon.

In the midst of my tears and reflecting on all that I have lost, I think about all that I have gained—a new found confidence in myself and the discovery of talents that I never knew existed. Prison broke my heart, made me strong, and changed my life for better. It gave me a new appreciation for something I never fully appreciated because it was given to me…FREEDOM.

I have developed an unshakeable relationship with God because it was here that He showed Himself to be trustworthy, loving, and faithful. Lord, thank you for Your undying love, never ending mercy, and unmerited grace. I called on You and You not only heard my cry but, You lifted me from a sea of despair and promised to carry my burdens if they ever became too heavy and You did. I reflect on all I have endured and I talk about how I walked through prison with grace, dignity, strength, and pride but, as I reflect on my journey to this day, I look back and only see the one set of footprints I have only heard about and all I can do is praise You.

I have forged awesome friendships with some people who have been great mentors to me; I learned that I am so much stronger and more resilient than I ever thought I could be; I discovered my purpose here and I have never been more excited about living my life. I gained compassion for

people that society may never accept.
I gained perspective and shed the bias ideologies' that are bred in society by people who will never understand what life behind bars is like.

I have a respect for the women here who won't ever breathe one breath of freedom again because I walked six years in their shoes and even though my freedom in five hours will separate us…we will forever be bonded by the razor wire.

"Every finish line is the beginning of a whole new race."

A Wake-Up   'Free-Day' September 1st, 2011

IT'S OVER!!!

April Nachelle Barksdale

How Will They Remember Me?

When I finally take my last breath and my weary heart beats no more; how will they remember me?

Will they remember me as their daughter; or as a ward of the state?

Will they remember all of the love, the love I had for my mates; or will they remember the ones, that I almost came to hate?

Will they remember the good deeds that I did; or will they remember why I served a bid?

Will they remember the fights that I won; or will they remember my struggles?

Will they remember me as their birthmother; or just a deadbeat, who gave them to another?

Will they remember when I wished them well; or when I had enough and told them to, "Go to hell?"

Will they remember my faithfulness; or will they remember the divorce?

Will they remember my failures; or how I persistently stayed the course?

Will they remember my rise to the top; or will they remember my fall?

Will they remember my head hung low; or the times when I proudly stood tall?

Will they remember when I told the truth; or will they remember, all of the lies?

Will they remember my happiness; or the many tears that I cried?

Will they remember the life that I lived; or will they remember the way that I died?

Will they remember me, as an enemy; or as a sister and a friend?

All I care to be remembered for is that I lived to make amends;

And lived my life to the fullest, with no regrets in the end.

Epilogue

My first day of freedom was one filled with emotion. I changed into my release clothing and had no problems walking in the heels. (SMILE) There was even more paperwork and final checks through the NCIC (National Crime Information System) to make sure none of us had outstanding warrants or were wanted in another state. The wait was nerve wrecking. You would think the release area would've been filled with jubilation and excitement but, it was extremely quiet. We just wanted to go.

It was time to leave and I reached the window to where an officer was sitting. She asked me to state my name and SCDC#. My voice trembled as I responded to her commands and the gate to freedom was opened to me.

The ride home was not as exciting as I thought it would be because I suffered from extreme car sickness that lasted for over a month so, I rode everywhere with my eyes closed.

I spent my first weekend home with my children who kept staring at me in disbelief that I was really there. My sister came from Philadelphia and my aunt and cousin came from out of town as well. It felt so good to be home.

The Monday after my release I started the job I applied for at a fast food restaurant...an industry I hadn't worked in since I was 16. It was surreal to be out and about with people. They would all be smiling and talking to me never knowing the hell I had just left behind.

I started a group on Facebook called, 'Beyond the RazorWire' as a place where former inmates (women) from the South Carolina Department of Corrections could keep in touch with, support, encourage, and share resources with the people we forged relationships with while incarcerated. As of the printing of this book, there are almost 500 proud members.

Prison ministry is my passion and it is my desire to see that all returning citizens (I don't like to use the word ex-offender) remain free for life. There is a quotation by Nelson Mandela that describes my journey best:

"I have walked that long road to freedom. I have tried not to falter; I have made missteps along the way. But I have discovered the secret that after climbing a great hill, one only finds that there are many more hills to climb. I have taken a moment here to rest, to steal a view of the glorious vista that surrounds me, to look back on the distance I have come. But I can only rest for a moment, for with freedom comes responsibilities, and I dare not linger, for my long walk is not ended."
—*Nelson Mandela*

ABOUT THE AUTHOR

April Nachelle Barksdale is a native South Carolinian and currently resides in Simpsonville, SC with her husband Bernard and her children; Jalen, Jasmine, and Jayla.

After her release, she started a Facebook group, *'Beyond the RazorWire'*, a place where formerly incarcerated women could keep in touch with, encourage, and support one another on their quest to remain free for life. She organized *Beyond the RazorWire* into a full-time prison ministry under her organization,

'C.H.A.R.I.S' Ministries (Complete Healing And Re-entry Into Society).
She is currently working on her next book,
'He Calls You Beloved: Rediscovering Your Identity in Christ'.

For Information regarding speaking engagements, 'He Calls You Beloved Workshops', or to contact the author please email correspondence to:

aprilbarksdale@yahoo.com

Or visit her on the web for exciting updates and news.

http://aprilbarksdaleauthor.wix.com/niara

Made in the USA
Middletown, DE
14 April 2025

74297621R00066